GET YOUR HOUSE IN ORDER

*The Basics of Financial Management
for Nonprofit Organizations and
Religious Institutions*

Dr. Ram'on O. Wideman

Anointed Business Solutions

Columbia

First printing

ISBN-13: 978-1500780944
PUBLISHED BY ANOINTED BUSINESS
SOLUTIONS, LLC
www.anointed-business-solutions.com
Columbia

Printed in the United States of America

Acknowledgements

First and foremost, I give honor, glory, praise, and worship to the trinity representation of God for making this accomplishment possible in my life. Without His constant, love, guidance, direction, and forgiveness, none of this would be possible. I am forever indebted with gratitude and servitude.

I also want to thank and honor my parents, the late Willie James and Bettye Jo Smith Wideman for their unconditional love and support and for setting the foundations of my life upon which I now stand as a husband, father, minister, and leader for social change. You have both meant and continue to mean so much to me and I could never repay you for your sacrifices, even unto death. I pray this makes you both proud and I carry each of you with me daily until we meet again in the sweet by and by.

I also wish to express my appreciation and thankfulness for my in-laws, Artie

Mae Ellis and the late James Ellis for taking me as your own son and always believing in me. You too have both meant and continue to mean more to me than you will ever know. I feel blessed to have and to have had you both in my life respectively.

I want to further express my love and gratitude to my brother, Willie James Wideman, Jr., and my sister, Zabeth Verlette Wideman Shepard. Both of you are lights in my life. I love you.

Last but not least, I thank the two most special people in my life – my beautiful and loving wife, Nevasha Shontae Ellis Wideman and my artistic, talented, and precious daughter Javiânce Elizabeth-Nicole Wideman. You both are my world and without you, there is no me. I could not have done this without your patience, understanding, commitment, and sacrifice. For these reasons amongst many, many others "I love you both…more than love!

GET YOUR HOUSE IN ORDER

*The Basics of Financial Management
for Nonprofit Organizations and
Religious Institutions*

Table of Contents

Introduction

In today's society, it is more important than ever for businesses to keep accurate financial records. The same holds true for nonprofit organizations and religious institutions, both of which have fallen under immense scrutiny from donors and regulatory bodies since the enactment of the Sarbanes-Oxley legislation in 2002. This scrutiny has been heighten even more for organizations of a charitable, philanthropic, or faith-based nature since the economic downtown that began in 2009.

One of the major challenges facing nonprofit and religious organizations concerning the management of their fiscal affairs is the ability to attract and retain competent professional financial staff members. Oftentimes, these organizations are faced with budget constraints that only enable them to secure the services of entry-level persons to fill jobs that require mid-career to executive level skill-sets. As a result, these organizations face constant turnover in their financial staffing and they are never able to truly build a sound operating base with fixed policies and procedures in place, primarily because they are ever-changing along with the fluctuations in their fiscal management infrastructure.

This challenge is further compounded for religious organizations in that their primary purpose in adopting business principles is only to achieve God's will and to grow his kingdom by the guidelines and stipulations that have been set forth by man. The scriptural reference for this philosophy is found in 1 Corinthians 14: 40; "Let all things be done decently and in order"; which is preceded by 1 Corinthians chapters 12 and 13 which offer instructions for the use of spiritual gifts, the representation of the body of Christ, and the establishment of protocol in the Church. It is important to remember; however, that the church is not a business, but it must at all times represents the body of Christ through ministry and service. This philosophy is one of the basic principles of kingdom building. Therefore, leaders, staff, and members have a moral obligation to be responsible stewards and to be accountable for the assets they hold in trust as representatives of God's kingdom on Earth.

Given that nonprofit and religious organizations primarily operate on the basis of gifts and funding from individuals and agencies, leaders of these different, yet very similar organizations serve as the stewards of these resources. Being responsible stewards entails using the resources entrusted to us in order to achieve the purpose for which they were given in the first place. For nonprofit organizations, the objective is to deliver quality services efficiently and effectively to the target population. In religious institutions, the primary aim is to advance the word and will of God. This brief handbook was written as a guide for both nonprofit organizations and religious institutions to use as a resource in order to accomplish their respective goals. To this end, it is my hope that the content that follows is insightful, meaningful, impactful, and most important, beneficial. Onward with the journey…

Accountability

The definition of accountability is responsibility to someone or for some activity; a form of trustworthiness; the trait of being answerable to someone for something or being responsible for one's conduct. Taking this definition into consideration automatically brings three (3) general questions to mind:

1. Who are you accountable to?

2. Why are you accountable?

3. How are you accountable?

As mentioned earlier, nonprofit organizations primarily operate on the basis of gifts from individuals, corporations and foundations. As such, managers of nonprofit organizations hold those gifts as stewards for their members, their clients and their communities. To this end, leaders of nonprofit organizations have a moral obligation to be responsible stewards and to be accountable for those assets. Furthermore, the tax-exempt status and the deductibility of contributions to nonprofit organizations brings with it an additional legal obligation to be accountable for the assets these organizations hold in trust.

The same holds true for religious organizations. These institutions primarily operate on the basis of gifts from individuals, referred to in the business world as giving units. To this end, leaders of religious organizations serve as the stewards of these gifts on behalf of God, the membership, and the surrounding communities they minister to. Therefore, leaders and members have a moral obligation to be responsible stewards and to be accountable for the assets they hold in trust as representatives of God's kingdom on Earth.

Nonprofit organizations and religious institutions exercise their stewardship responsibilities by ensuring that the assets belonging to their organizations are not converted to private use, but are used wisely to further the purpose for which the institutions were created and for which the funds were contributed. Moreover, nonprofit organizations and religious institutions also exercise their stewardship responsibilities by ensuring that they accurately report the assets they have received and how those assets are used.

Resource Utilization

Perhaps the most important component of resource utilization is budgeting. Budgeting is a part of sound planning. It is a back and forth process. The steps in the budgeting process are as follows:

1. Develop the "dream" program plan.

2. Price the "dream" program plan.

3. Take a realistic look at how much money you can expect to bring in.

4. Go back and rework the program plan.

5. Keep going back and forth until you have a program plan that is balanced with an income plan and an expenditure plan.

There are some important principles to follow when going through the budgeting process:

➤ Include both income and expenses. Budgets are not just about what you will spend. They are equally about realistic estimates of income.

➢ Be realistic.

Question: If you only raised $25,000 in non-grant donations this year, why do you think you can raise $100,000 next year?

➢ Your budget should include a reasonable estimate for a "worst case" scenario.

Question: What happens if you do not get a grant renewal you were counting on?

Question: What if the roof falls in and we have to replace it?

Assets Protection

Internal controls are procedures to protect the assets of the corporation. They are clearly defined procedures and policies for handling contributions and making expenditures, purchasing and keeping assets like supplies and equipment, and the making of investments.

There are six (6) key elements of a strong system of internal controls:

1. Employing competent, trustworthy people with clear lines of authority and responsibility.

2. Having adequate separation of duties.

3. Having proper procedures for authorizing business transactions.

4. Maintaining adequate documents and records.
5. Having appropriate physical controls over assets and records.

6. Conducting independent checks on performance.

One person should not be getting the mail, opening the envelopes, making the deposits and keeping the books. One person should not write the checks, sign the checks and keep the books. In small nonprofits with few employees, separation of duties may seem impossible; however, it is possible to contract with outside accounting firms or utilize your Board of Directors.

Risk Management

Things beyond our control happen. Burglars strike. Clients get hurt while we are providing them services. We mess up and do not file forms we are supposed to file. Stewardship requires that we identify and assess the risk that we face.

Donors do not give gifts and contributions to replace stolen computers, to fund defense of lawsuits, or to pay IRS penalties. Therefore, leaders of nonprofit organizations and religious institutions have to develop policies and practices to reduce risks (i.e. establish internal controls, protect against injury, ensure legal compliance, etc).

To protect nonprofit organizations and religious institutions even further from risk, leaders of these entities must make sure that these establishments are adequately insured by securing appropriate insurances such as:

➢ General Liability Insurance – This is coverage to defend against claims, indemnify (i.e. pay) all sums for which the insured is held liable, and to settle all reasonable claims.

➢ Automobile Insurance – This is coverage to protect vehicles belonging to the organization/institution, drivers of those vehicles on behalf of the organization/institution, and other motorist who may be affected by collision with vehicles belonging to the organization/institution.

➢ Workers Compensation Insurance – This is coverage providing wage replacement and medical benefits to employees injured in the course of employment in exchange for mandatory abandonment of the employee's right to sue his or her employer for the offense of negligence.

➢ Fidelity (Bonding) Insurance – This is coverage that protects policyholders for losses they incur as a result of fraudulent acts by specified individuals. It usually insures a business for losses caused by the dishonest acts of its employees.

➤ Property Insurance – This is coverage that provides protection against most risks to property, such as fire, theft and some weather damage.

➤ Directors and Officers Insurance – This is coverage that is payable to the directors and officers of a company, or to the organization(s) itself, as indemnification (reimbursement) for losses or advancement of defense costs in the event an insured suffers such a loss as a result of a legal action brought for alleged wrongful acts in their capacity as directors and officers. Such coverage can extend to defense costs arising out of criminal and regulatory investigations/trials as well; in fact, often civil and criminal actions are brought against directors/officers simultaneously.

➤ Professional Liability Insurance – Also known as Errors & Omissions insurance, this is coverage that protects professional advice- and service-providing individuals and companies from bearing the full cost of defending against a negligence claim made by a client, and damages awarded in such a civil lawsuit. The coverage focuses on alleged failure to perform on the part of, financial loss caused by, and error or omission in the service or product sold by the policyholder. These are potential causes for legal action that would not be covered by a more general liability insurance policy which addresses more direct forms of harm. Professional liability coverage sometimes also provides for the defense costs, including when legal action turns out to be groundless. Coverage does not include criminal prosecution, nor a wide range of potential liabilities under civil law that are not enumerated in the policy, but which may be subject to other forms of insurance.

Bookkeeping 101

Bookkeeping defined is the task of recording amounts, dates and sources of all business revenue, gain, expense, and loss transactions. Bookkeeping is the starting point of the accounting process. Bookkeeping is done and financial statements are prepared so that organizations and institutions can:

1. Better manage resources in order to more effectively meet our organizational purposes.

2. Comply with legal reporting requirements to the regulatory bodies (i.e. IRS, the Secretary of State, the Department of Revenue, the Employment Security Commission, etc).

3. Account to the public on our use of tax-subsidized contributions.

4. Account to members and donors on how we have spent the contributions they gave.

In order to initially establish a set of books, one would ideally sit down with an accountant to create a chart of accounts and a system for recording financial information before the first dime is ever received. Most small organizations/institutions, however, do not have an accountant. Therefore, the Executive Director/Pastor/Business Manager and the Treasurer have to figure it out. A relatively inexpensive computer program like QuickBooks can make this whole process much easier.

For small organizations, the books do not need to be complex. The chart of accounts should be concise and should only include accounts and departments that will aid in effectively managing the financials of the organization/institution.

Creating a Budget

The steps of the budgeting process were discussed earlier in the text, but how is that actual budget pulled together in a presentable format? Take the following example.

Ex: You will receive revenue in the amount of $50,000 from donations and contributions, $35,000 from Foundation A, $12,500 from Foundation B, and $7,500 from Foundation C for the current fiscal year. You have the following expenses: Salaries (Executive Director $35,000, Secretary $14,750) Fringe benefits at 10% of total salaries. Utilities at $20,000 (i.e. electric, water, sewer, etc.). Rent at $500/month (for a 12 month period). Travel and conference expenses at $4,025. Accounting and audit expenses at $15,000. Contingency at 5% (this is money set aside for worst case scenarios as discussed earlier).

Using this information, we can fill in the following template:

Revenue:

Donations/Contributions	$	50,000
Foundation A	$	35,000
Foundation B	$	12,500
Foundation C	$	7,500
Total Revenue:	$	**105,000**

Expenses:

Salaries	$	49,750
Fringe Benefits	$	4,975
Utilities	$	20,000
Rent	$	6,000
Travel and Conference	$	4,025
Accounting and Audit	$	15,000
Contingency	$	5,250
Total Expenses:	**$**	**105,000**

Creating a Chart of Accounts

A chart of accounts (COA) can also be created using the information from the budget example. Each revenue source should be set up as a department. Note that departments should only be set up for items you wish to tract a category of expenditures for. As a general rule, revenue streams should always be set up as departments in order to appropriately track income versus expenditures.

Each expense account should be assigned an account number. Start with 100 for departments and number each department in increments of 100. Start with 1000 for accounts and number each account in increments of 1000.

Revenue:	**COA Departments:**
Donations/Contributions	<u>100</u>
Foundation A	<u>200</u>
Foundation B	<u>300</u>
Foundation C	<u>400</u>

Expenses:	**COA Account #s:**
Salaries	<u>1000</u>
Fringe Benefits	<u>2000</u>
Utilities	<u>3000</u>
Rent	<u>4000</u>
Travel and Conference	<u>5000</u>
Accounting and Audit	<u>6000</u>
Contingency	<u>7000</u>

Creating a Budget and Chart of Accounts Matrix

Now examine the following matrix to see how the budget and chart of accounts interact. Note the allocation methodology at the bottom of the matrix. The allocation methodology represents the proportion of funding received from each funding source with regard to total revenue. These are the percentage allocations you should use throughout the fiscal year to charge costs associated with budgeted expense line items (i.e. if your annual audit costs $5,000, you will bill 48% to Member Contributions, 33% to Foundation A, 12% to Foundation B and 7% to Foundation C).

Line Item	Account #	Donations/ Contributions 100	Foundation A 200	Foundation B 300	Foundation C 400	Total
Salaries	1000	$23,880.00	$16,420.00	$5,970.00	$3,480.00	$49,750.00
Fringe Benefits	2000	$2,388.00	$1,642.00	$597.00	$348.00	$4,975.00
Utilities	3000	$9,600.00	$6,600.00	$2,400.00	$1,400.00	$20,000.00
Rent	4000	$2,880.00	$1,980.00	$720.00	$420.00	$6,000.00
Travel and Conference	5000	$1,932.00	$1,328.00	$483.00	$282.00	$4,025.00
Accounting and Audit	6000	$7,200.00	$4,950.00	$1,800.00	$1,050.00	$15,000.00
Contingency	7000	$2,120.00	$2,080.00	$630.00	$420.00	$5,250.00
Total	N/A	$50,000.00	$35,000.00	$12,600.00	$7,400.00	$105,000.00
Allocation Methodology		48%	33%	12%	7%	100%

(Department Name and #)

The Audit Process and Public Expectations

After the business cycle for the fiscal year has come to an end, the annual audit process may come into play. An audit is not something that is necessarily required by law; however, it is a good business practice to have one routinely to make sure that the financial information and the integrity of the financial data an organization/institution shares with its supporters is accurate and fairly presented according to Generally Accepted Accounting Principles (GAAP). Additionally, some funders and lenders may require an organization/institution to conduct an audit of its financial records as part of the funding/lending agreement. In these cases, the audit process is necessary to ensure compliance and continuation of the arrangement.

There are several public expectations of the audit process. First, it is expected that audit organizations are independent. This means that auditors should not perform management functions or make management decisions for the organizations/institutions they audit. Second, it is expected that auditors remain objective throughout the audit process. In other words, auditors should not audit their own work or provide non-audit services in situations where the amounts or services involved are significant/material to the subject matter of the audit.

Audit Controls, Internal Controls, and Independence Issues

Regarding audit controls, personnel who perform certain non-audit services would be precluded from performing related audit work. Additionally, the auditor's work cannot be reduced beyond the level that would be appropriate if the non-audit work was performed by another unrelated party. Furthermore, certain documentation and quality assurance requirements must be met (i.e. source of documentation, validity of documentation, etc.).

Concerning internal controls within the organization/institution being audited, the accounting department must be adequately staffed to ensure appropriate separation of duties. The accounting department must also be solely responsible for maintaining and preparing the accounting records to be audited. Lastly, management of the organization/institution being audited must assumes full responsibility for all decisions affecting its financial statements.

An audit organization's independence to perform an audit is impaired if it maintains or prepares the audited entity's basic accounting records. An audit organization's independence to perform an audit is also impaired if it maintains or takes responsibility for basic financial or other records that the audit organization will audit. Moreover, an audit organization's independence to perform an audit is impaired if it posts transactions to the entity's financial records or to other records that subsequently provide data to the entity's financial records. These are all safeguards auditors must take in order to be able to issue an uncompromised opinion regarding the accuracy, validity, and integrity of the financial information and data maintained and presented by the organization/institution under audit.

Developing Draft Financial Statements and Notes

For auditors, developing draft financial statements and notes pertaining to the financial statements is viewed as technical assistance and part of the audit process. Auditors must; however, be careful not to actually construct the accounting records of the organization/institution under audit.

The draft financial statements must:

> ➢ Be based on a trial balance.

> ➢ Be provided by management using appropriate books and records that balance, or

> ➢ Be prepared by auditors when their work to prepare the trail balance is technical formatting in nature and uses management's chart of accounts.

Additionally, the draft financial statements must be reviewed and approved by the management of the audited organizations/institution, who must have adequate knowledge to evaluate the statements and to take responsibility for the result. Furthermore, a management representation letter should be included, acknowledging the auditor's role and management's review, approval, and responsibility for the financial statements and notes.

The 990

The 990 is basically the tax return for charitable organizations. It includes information on the filing entity's mission, programs, and finances. Most federally tax-exempt organizations are required to file a 990 annually. All 501(c)(3) private foundations, regardless of their income, are also required to file a 990 annually. Organizations not required to file a 990 annually include:

➢ Nonprofits that have not received tax-exempt status from the IRS.

➢ Most faith-based organizations.

➢ State institutions.

➢ Subsidiary organizations covered under a group return filed by the parent organization.

There is no universal "due date" for 990s to be submitted to the Internal revenue Service (IRS). Instead, organizations who are required to file a 990 must do so by the 15th day of the 5th month after its fiscal year ends.

990s are often prepared as the final step in the audit process as the reviewed statements are needed to fill in the financial portion of the return. 990s can be filed electronically or by mail. Charitable organizations who are required to file a 990 and who do not do so for three consecutive years will automatically lose their tax-exempt status with the IRS.

Review and Conclusion

Accountability is akin to responsibility. Managers and officers of nonprofit organizations and religious institutions have a fiduciary responsibility to safeguard the assets of those establishments. Furthermore, managers and officers of nonprofit organizations and religious institutions have a fiduciary responsibility to ensure that the resources of their organizations are utilized to the maximum benefit of their clients, customers and members.

In order to meet their fiduciary responsibilities, managers and officers of nonprofit organizations and religious institutions must develop sound financial practices and strategies to ensure efficient and effective operations. This entails have sound policies and procedures as well as a clear understanding of day-to-day operations and the risks associated with being in business. Therefore, it is of the utmost importance to managers and officers of nonprofit organizations and religious institutions to stay continually abreast of their respective current financial positions in order that they may be adequately equipped to make reasonable decisions in the present and realistic forecasts for the future.

About the Author

Dr. Ram'on O. Wideman is a native of Greenwood, South Carolina. He is the son of the late Willie James Wideman, Sr. and the late Bettye Jo Smith Wideman. He is an honors graduate of Greenwood High School and a Magna Cum Laude honors graduate of the University of South Carolina with a Bachelor of Arts degree in Political Science and a concentration in Public Administration. Ram'on also holds a Master of Arts degree in Business Management, a Master of Business Administration degree, and a Master of Health Administration degree from Webster University, as well as a Doctorate in Business Administration degree from Ashley University with a focus in Finance and Accounting.

Ram'on is a business and finance professional. He is the President/CEO of Anointed Business Solutions, LLC as well as an ordained minister with years of concentrated experience in managing the fiscal affairs of religious organizations. Ram'on also teaches and gives presentations throughout the state of South Carolina on financial matters affecting Christians and faith-based institutions. He lives in Columbia, South Carolina with his wife and daughter. This is his third book.